W9-AYG-034

Publisher: Spurlock Photography, Inc.
Managing/Photo Editor: Brian Spurlock,
   Spurlock Photography, Inc.
Editor: Jai Giffin, Host Communications, Inc.
Design: Bob Slater, Host Communications, Inc.
Production: Host Communications, Inc. ▪ 904 North
   Broadway ▪ Lexington, KY 40505 (859) 226-4510

Photographers: Tom DiPace, Michael Hebert, Don
   Kelly, Joe Robbins, Brian Spurlock, Sally Spurlock.

Front Cover Photos: Brian Spurlock
Front Cover Design: Bob Slater, Host
Communications, Inc.
Back Cover Photos: Brian Spurlock
Photomosaics: patented by Robert Silvers/
Runaway Technology

Orders for this publication can be made by
contacting:
Spurlock Photography, Inc.
P.O. Box 406
Fishers, Indiana 46038-0406
Phone: (317) 841-2857
Fax: (317) 841-2868

The cover price is $11.99 (Indiana residents add 5%
sales tax). Payment can be made by money order,
cashier's check, VISA, MasterCard or Discover Card.

The rights to the name, likeness and signature of
Jeff Gordon and the likeness of the #24 DuPont
Chevrolet are granted under license from JG
Motorsports, Inc. ©2002 JG Motorsports, Inc.

NASCAR is a registered trademark of the National
Association for Stock Car Auto Racing.

© 1997 Brian Spurlock

ALL-AMERICAN HERO

By Brian Spurlock

Jeff Gordon has been a successful race car driver almost his entire life. Jeff won three sprint car track championships before he was old enough to get a driver's license. By the time he graduated from high school, he had already won more than 100 races. It seems that he is always the youngest or first to accomplish a number of feats. In 1990, he won the USAC Midget Championship and, at age 19, he became the youngest Midget class champion ever. At 20, he became the youngest driver to win the USAC Silver Crown division. He holds the NASCAR record of seven road course victories and, at the age of 30, has won four Winston Cup Championships.

© 2001 All Photos By Brian Spurlock

To put it in perspective, Richard Petty was 27 when he won his first Winston Cup Championship. Petty and Dale Earnhardt own the record, each having won seven championships — Jeff is well on his way to reaching that mark.

Jeff has further established himself as an elite driver by winning almost 20 percent of the races he starts and finishing in the top five around 50 percent of the time.

I grew up within walking distance of the Indianapolis Motor Speedway and I really started following Jeff's career when he won the Inaugural Brickyard 400 in 1994. Over the course of his career, I have taken approximately 20,000 photos relating to Jeff Gordon and the No. 24 car. You can imagine how difficult the decision was to narrow this book to about 200 photos of Jeff's illustrious career. I hope you will enjoy this comprehensive photo review of Jeff Gordon and his Winston Cup career.

As impressive as Jeff's racing skills and ability to win on the track are his conduct and professionalism out of the car. I have seen him sign countless autographs, do endless numbers of interviews, whether he has had a good day or not, and help raise money for charities. I truly believe that ability may get someone to the top, but it takes character to keep you there. The night before the September 2001 race in Dover, while I was having dinner with Robbie Loomis, Jeff Gordon's crew chief, Robbie told the story of how Jeff was not allowed in the garage area at Dover because he was not carrying his NASCAR credentials. After the terrorists' attacks, security was tightened and even Jeff Gordon in his DuPont racing suit was not getting in the garage area without his NASCAR identification card. Since there were rumors of possible terrorists having stolen pilot uniforms, NASCAR was taking no chances of anybody impersonating drivers to get in restricted areas. I think if someone tried to get behind the steering wheel of the No. 24 car other than Jeff Gordon that you would know right away that it's impossible to impersonate his incredible driving skills.

In my conversation with Loomis, I brought up that Jeff had spoken at the Billy Graham Crusade in Indianapolis and given his testimony about being a born-again Christian. Loomis had so many nice things to say about Jeff, but the one statement that really stood out was one concerning Jeff's personal relationship with Jesus Christ: "Jeff not only talks the talk, but he walks the walk."

The year of 2001 has been marked with the tragedies of Dale Earnhardt's death and the terrorist attacks. Life is fragile, and there is no certainty of tomorrow or what the future may hold. No matter if you would have the fame and fortune of Jeff Gordon, the most important thing in life is to know where you may spend eternity. Jeff Gordon, as well as many of the other NASCAR drivers, know this because they have accepted by faith what is preached in the Motor Racing Outreach services held each Sunday morning before the race starts. The Bible verse John 3:16 says it best: "For God so loved the world that he gave his only begotten Son, that whosoever believeth in him should not perish but have everlasting life."

I leave you with this one thought. John Wooden, the legendary basketball coach from UCLA, speaks each year at the McDonald's High School All-American banquet for the top high school basketball players in the country. He almost always quotes this phrase, which is a good motto to live by whether you are an All-American basketball player or an All-American Hero such as Jeff Gordon.

Four things a man must learn to do
If he would make his life more true
To think without confusion clearly,
To love his fellow man sincerely,
To act from honest motives purely,
To trust in God and Heaven securely.

Special thanks to Jeff Gordon for officially endorsing this book and for a dynamic career that has truly been a pleasure to photograph. Special thanks to HOST Communications for their design and help in putting this book together, and to my attorney and father, Ben Spurlock, for his help in handling legal contracts and providing guidance to make the right decisions in life. Special thanks to my wife, Sally, for her support and love and keeping the family together while I was on the road working on this book.

"
Jeff not only talks the talk, but he walks the walk.
"
— *Robbie Loomis*

Jeff poses after winning the pole for the 1995 Brickyard 400. © 1995 Brian Spurlock

$13.99

$11.99

jeff GORDON
PHOTO TRIBUTE TO A CHAMPION

COLLECTOR'S EDITION

Price includes shipping and handling.
Orders can be obtained by contacting:

Spurlock Photography, Inc.
P.O. Box 406
Fishers, Indiana 46038-0406
Phone: (317) 841-2857
Fax: (317) 841-2868

Back cover available
as a poster in 2002.

Payable by money order, cashier's check, VISA, MasterCard or Discover Card.
Indiana residents please add 5% sales tax.

The 24 car makes a
pit stop at Martinsville.

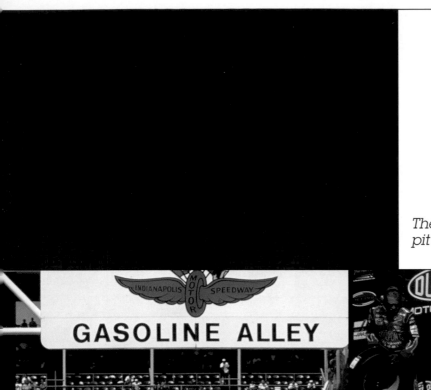

The world's greatest drivers have
entered Gasoline Alley for nearly
a century.

© All photos by Brian Spurlock

Gordon salutes the fans on his victory lap at the inaugural Brickyard 400 in 1994.

Jeff hugs the trophy after becoming a two-time winner of the Brickyard 400 in 1998.

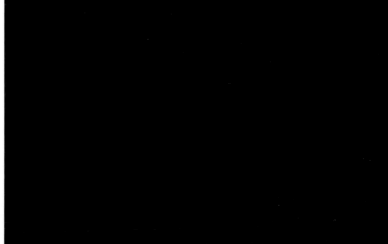

Memory Lane

Gordon has been strapping into race cars since age 5 and by age 8 had won his first Quarter Midget championship.

© 1999 Brian Spurlock

In 1999, the Rainbow Warrior passes by en route to his second of three victories at Sears Point.

© 1999 Brian Spurlock

"THROUGH THESE DOORS PASS THE WORLD'S BEST DRIVERS"

Winston Cup Champions Dale Earnhardt, Jeff Gordon and Bobby Labonte leaving the garage area at Charlotte.

© 1997 Brian Spurlock

Gordon arrives
at the office.

© 1997 Brian Spurlock

© 1997 Brian Spurlock

Gordon discusses race set up with crew chief Ray Evernham. These two teamed up to win three Winston Cup championships.

© 1997 Brian Spurlock

Gordon meditates in the garage area at Fontana. He later went on to become the inaugural winner of the California 500.

© 1997 Brian Spurlock

© 1998 Brian Spurlock

The image of Jeff Gordon is synonymous with winning.
At 30, he is the winningest active driver with 58 wins
(seventh all-time). Jeff averages a victory every five starts

In 1997, Gordon won 10 races and the Winston Cup title.

© 1997 Brian Spurlock

© 1996 Brian Spurlock

A familiar sight at Sears Point has been Winston Cup competitors playing follow the leader with Jeff Gordon.

© 1999 Brian Spurlock

After winning at Sears Point in June 1998, Gordon went on to win four-consecutive races (Pocono, Indianapolis, Watkins Glen and Michigan).

© 1998 Brian Spurlock

"Air Gordon" flies through turn three at Sears Point and
ends the day with a refreshing drink in victory lane

© 1999 Brian Spurlock

© 1999 Brian Spurlock

Shades of victory.

© 1997 Brian Spurlock

© 2000 Brian Spurlock

Jeff pushes his car through the qualifying line at Martinsville.

After qualifying at Martinsville, Gordon watches as the crew prepares the car for race day.

© 2000 Brian Spurlock

Gordon prepares to do battle
on a Sunday afternoon.

© 1998 Brian Spurlock

Before the start of the race at Dover, Jeff and Brooke share a moment in prayer with Max Helton of Motor Racing Outreach.

© 1996 Brian Spurlock

Jeff prepares for the start of the 1997
Brickyard 400. In 1997, he became the
only driver in NASCAR history to exceed
$4 million in regular season earnings.

© 1997 Michael Hebert/
Spurlock Photography, Inc.

"I only know one way to race and that's to go all out for the win."

© All Photos By Brian Spurlock

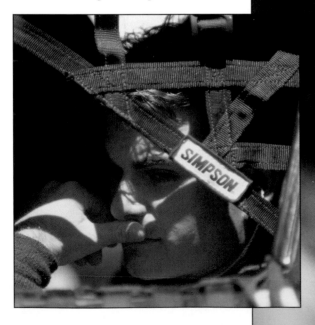

Corporate sponsors and bright colors have put NASCAR in the spotlight.

© 1999 Brian Spurlock

Life in the
fast lane.

© 1998 Brian Spurlock

Fans gather as the No. 24 Peanuts car is pushed to the starting grid for the 2000 Brickyard 400.

© 2000 Brian Spurlock

*Gordon and teammate Ricky Craven
lead the pack through turn one at
New Hampshire.*

© 1998 Brian Spurlock

More than 350,000 fans watch as the local hero from Pittsboro, Indiana, leads the field into turn one at the start of the Brickyard 400.

© 1999 Brian Spurlock

Throughout his Winston Cup career, Gordon has been a constant in the media spotlight. He finishes in the top five in more than 50 percent of the races and places in the top 10 more than 65 percent of the time. His career earnings total more than $41 million.

© All Photos By Brian Spurlock

Jeff and Brooke celebrate the Winston Million at Darlington in 1997. Bill Elliott, in 1985, was the only other driver to win this coveted prize.

© 1997 Brian Spurlock

© 1997 Brian Spurlock

© 1997 Brian Spurlock

Ray Evernham was about the only person around the track to stay within reach of "Flash" Gordon in 1997. Gordon was "on fire" that year with 10 wins, including the Daytona 500 and Charlotte 600. Here he's shown celebrating after clinching the Winston Million bonus at Darlington.

© 2001 Brian Spurlock

© 2001 Brian Spurlock

Exhausted and cooling off after his win at Sears Point in 1998.

Gordon has won three inaugural races — The Brickyard 400 (bottom photo), California 500 (photo on left) and the Protection One 400 in Kansas City. On winning his first Brickyard 400 ... "Winning it was one of the greatest feelings I ever had in racing. I'll never forget it."

© All Photos By
Brian Spurlock

The thrill of victory after winning the 1997 Daytona 500 (below). Ricky Craven showers Gordon with champagne after Hendrick Motorsports finishes 1-2-3 at Daytona.

© 1997 Brian Spurlock

© 1997 Brian Spurlock

© 1995 Don Kelly/
Spurlock Photography, Inc.

The Gordons celebrate the
1995 and 1997 Winston
Cup Championships.

© 1997 Brian Spurlock

© 1998 Brian Spurlock

Gordon kisses the famous yard of bricks at the start/finish line at the Indianapolis Motor Speedway.

© 1998 Brian Spurlock

© 1998 Brian Spurlock

Jeff celebrates the largest recorded payday in racing history by winning $1.6 million in the 1998 Brickyard 400.

*The Hoosier favorite and people's champion
takes a victory lap after receiving the $1 million
Winston No Bull 5 bonus.*

Winston
5
2206
4700
Loomis, Fargo & Co.
98
LF&Co

© 1998 Sally Spurlock/Spurlock Photography, Inc.

Jeff Gordon continued his domination during the 1999 season by winning his second Daytona 500. With seven victories in 1999, he won more races (47) from 1995-99 than any other Winston Cup driver.

© 1999 Photos By Tom DiPace

NASCAR Winston Cup
2001 Champion

2001 CHAMPION

NASCAR WINSTON CUP

2001 C

© 2001 Brian Spurlock

NASCAR

PAY TO THE
ORDER OF

Three M...ix H... Thousand DOL

MEMO   CH...NSHIP

NASCAR
Winston Cup
Champion

3,600,000

FROM   Winst
R.J. Reynolds Tobacc

NASCAR W...
JEF

Gordon and crew chief Robbie Loomis celebrate their 2001 Winston Cup Championship.

Martinsville ...
spun and
won ...

Celebrates win at California.

Leaps from his car after capturing Hendrick Motorsports' 100th victory at Michigan.

1997
NASCAR WINSTON CUP CHAMPION
JEFF GORDON

One of four NASCAR Winston
Cup Championship trophies.

© All photos By Brian Spurlock

© All Photos By Brian Spurlock

© Brian Spurlock (9); Joe Robbins (1); Michael Hebert (1)

© 1999 Brian Spurlock

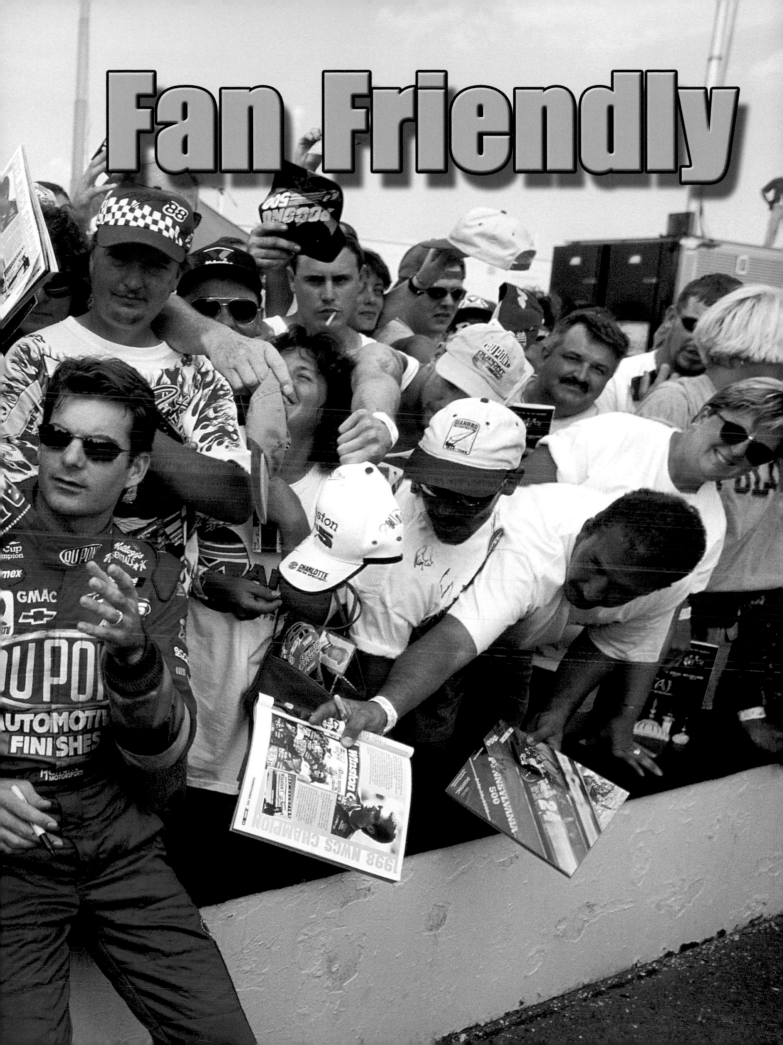

Fan Friendly

© All Photos By Brian Spurlock

© All Photos By Brian Spurlock

© All Photos By Brian Spurlock

© All Photos By
Brian Spurlock

© All Photos By Brian Spurlock

© 2001 Brian Spurlock

2001 Bugs Bunny
Richmond

1999 NASCAR Racers
Homestead

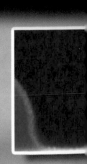

SPECIAL PAINT
SCH

2001 Pepsi
Talladega

2000 Silver Metallic
Daytona

2000 Busch Pepsi
Michigan

2000 Peanuts
Brickyard

© Brian Spurlock (6); Tom DiPace (1)

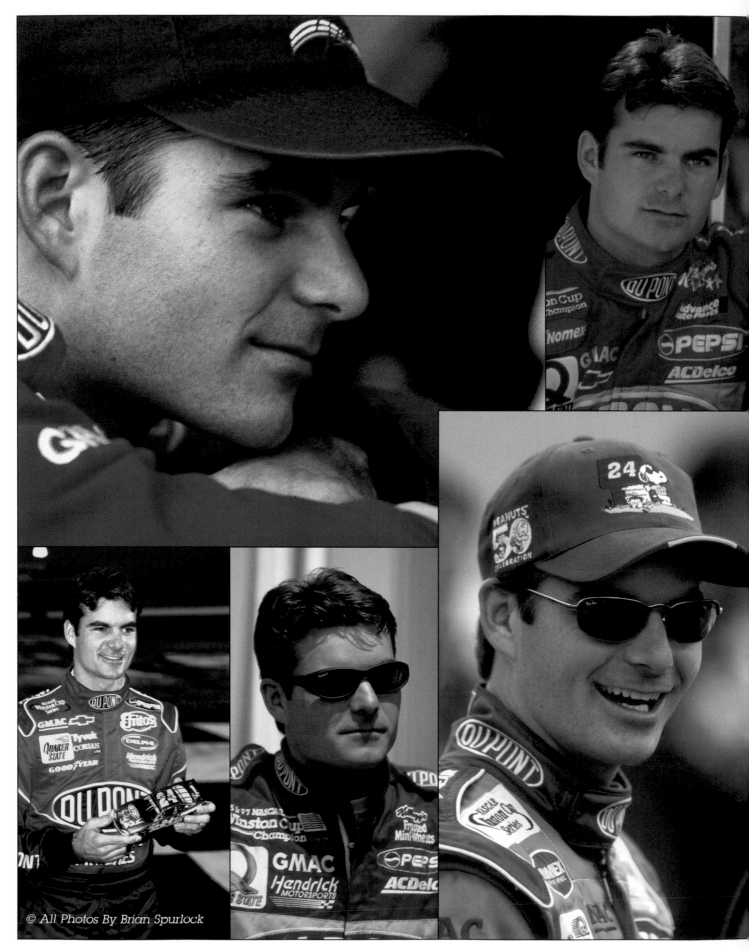

© All Photos By Brian Spurlock

Jeff & Brooke

Jeff and Brooke share a laugh before the Chicago race.

rain•X
SLICK
50
1-800-MARROW-2

DUPO

PEPSI

Fritos

EAGLE

GOOD/YEAR

LK-8

© 2001 Brian Spurlock

© 2001 Brian Spurlock

© 2000 Brian Spurlock

Jeff and Brooke in
a familiar place —
victory lane.

© 2001 Brian Spurlock

© 2001 Brian Spurlock

"Brooke helps me keep everything in perspective. She's not only my wife, she's my best friend."

© 2001 Brian Spurlock

© 1998 Brian Spurlock

A moment for their sponsors.

Brooke gives the champion a kiss in victory lane at Talladega.

Everyone is all smiles in victory lane at Michigan in 2001.

© All Photos By Brian Spurlock

© 1997 Brian
Spurlock

© 1997 Brian Spurlock

*Jeff helps Brooke from the
GTO after a lap around
Pocono during driver
introductions (right); while
Brooke helps Jeff into the car
at New Hampshire (above).*

© All Photos By Brian Spurlock

Jeff married former Miss Winston, Brooke Sealy, in November 1994.

© 1998 Brian Spurlock

"Show me the money."
The Gordons needed an
armored truck to carry their
$1.6 million winnings from
the 1998 Brickyard 400.

© 1997 Brian Spurlock

© All Photos By Brian Spurlock

2001 SEASON

*Gordon shows his excitement after passing
Ricky Rudd on the final lap to win the
Michigan 400.*

© 2001 Brian Spurlock

"Sometimes pure desire overcomes everything out there and you do everything it takes to get to victory lane."

— Jeff Gordon

© 2001 Brian Spurlock

"We've been competitve in every race this year. We're leading laps and putting ourselves in position to win races."

© 2001 Brian Spurlock

"I give a lot of credit to Robbie Loomis (crew chief). He wasn't afraid to make some big changes and go away from what had traditionally worked for the No. 24 car. That's exactly what we've had to do."

© 2001 Brian Spurlock

"Qualifying is so important because of track position and especially pit stall selection. It makes everything easier for the pit crew if you can get a stall that has an opening in front of or behind it."
— Jeff Gordon

© 2001 Brian Spurlock

"A lot of people have come and gone in this organization," said Gordon after Hendrick Motorsports' 100th victory at Michigan.

Hendrick
MOTORSPORTS
100
VICTORIES
1984 - 2001

© 2001 Brian Spurlock

"But Rick and I have maintained a great relationship both on and off the track."

"It's hard to imagine that I've won 58 races. It seems like yesterday when I got my first win in the 600. I guess we've just put the throttle down and never really looked back."

Jeff Gordon before the June race at Michigan.

© 2001 Brian Spurlock

The pit crew signals that they have 22 gallons of fuel in the car.

Jeff with sports legends Muhammed Ali and Cal Ripken Jr.

In 2001, Gordon won six poles and six races.

© 2001 Brian Spurlock

© 2001 Brian Spurlock

Gordon leads the field at the start of the Save Mart 350.

The Brickyard 400 celebration.

© All Photos By Brian Spurlock

With a win at Watkins Glen, Gordon became NASCAR's all-time leader in road course victories with seven.

Jeff wins the pole at Richmond.

What's Up Doc?

© 2001 Brian Spurlock (3); Joe Robbins (1)

At Dover, the No. 24 team shows its patriotism and pays its respect to the victims of the terrorist attacks on September 11.

© 2001 Brian Spurlock

Gordon hoists his fourth championship trophy. He is only one of three drivers to win more than three titles.

© 2001 Brian Spurlock

© 2001 Brian Spurlock

"He ain't heavy, he's my brother."

REFUSE TO LOSE

Date	Victory	Site

1992
No Wins

1993
No Wins

- Finished 14th in points

1994
| May 29 | Coca-Cola 600 | Charlotte |
| August 6 | Brickyard 400 | Indianapolis |

- Finished 8th in points

1995
February 26	Goodwrench 500	Rockingham
March 12	Purolator 500	Atlanta
April 2	Food City 500	Bristol
July 1	Pepsi 400	Daytona
July 9	Slick 50 300	Watkins Glen
September 3	Southern 500	Darlington
September 17	MBNA 500	Dover

- Winston Cup Champion

1996
March 3	Pontiac Excitement 400	Richmond
March 24	TranSouth Financial 400	Darlington
March 31	Food City 500	Bristol
June 2	Miller 500	Dover
June 16	UAW-GM 500	Pocono
July 28	DieHard 500	Talladega
September 1	Southern 500	Darlington
September 15	MBNA 500	Dover
September 22	Hanes 500	Martinsville
September 29	Holly Farms 400	North Wilkesboro

- Finished 2nd in points

1997
February 16	Daytona 500	Daytona
February 23	Goodwrench 400	Rockingham
April 13	Food City 500	Bristol
April 20	Goody's 500	Martinsville
May 25	Coca-Cola 600	Charlotte
June 8	Pocono 500	Pocono
June 22	California 500	Fontana
August 10	Bud at the Glen	Watkins Glen
August 31	Southern 500	Darlington
September 14	CMT 300	New Hampshire

- Winston Cup Champion

Date	Victory	Site

1998
February 22	Goodwrench 400	Rockingham
March 29	Food City 500	Bristol
May 24	Coca-Cola 600	Charlotte
June 28	Save Mart 350	Sears Point
July 26	Pennsylvania 500	Pocono
August 1	Brickyard 400	Indianapolis
August 9	Bud at the Glen	Watkins Glen
August 16	Pepsi 400	Michigan
August 30	CMT 300	New Hampshire
September 6	Southern 500	Darlington
October 17	Pepsi 400	Daytona
November 1	AC Delco 400	Rockingham
November 8	NAPA 500	Atlanta

- Winston Cup Champion

1999
February 14	Daytona 500	Daytona
March 14	Cracker Barrel 500	Atlanta
May 2	California 500	Fontana
June 27	Save Mart 350	Sears Point
August 15	Frontier at the Glen	Watkins Glen
October 3	NAPA Autocare 500	Martinsville
October 11	UAW-GM Quality 500	Charlotte

- Finished 7th in points

2000
August 16	DieHard 500	Talladega
June 25	Save Mart 350	Sears Point
September 9	Chevrolet Monte Carlo 400	Richmond

- Finished 9th in points

2001
March 4	UAW-Daimler-Chrysler 400	Las Vegas
June 3	MBNA 400	Dover
June 10	Kmart 400	Michigan
August 5	Brickyard 400	Indianapolis
August 12	Global Crossing at the Glen	Watkins Glen
September 30	Protection One 400	Kansas City

- Winston Cup Champion

CAREER STATISTICS

Year	Starts	Wins	Top 5	Top 10	Money Won	Poles
1992	1	0	0	0	$6,285	0
1993	30	0	7	11	$765,168	1
1994	31	2	7	14	$1,779,523	1
1995	31	7	17	23	$4,347,343	8
1996	31	10	21	24	$3,428,485	5
1997	32	10	22	23	$6,375,658	1
1998	33	13	26	28	$9,306,584	7
1999	34	7	18	21	$5,858,633	7
2000	34	3	11	22	$3,001,144	3
2001	36	6	18	24	$10,879,757	6
Totals	293	58	147	190	$45,748,580	39

2001
NASCAR WINSTON CUP CHAMPION
JEFF GORDON